The Monster in the Cave

A Play

Written by Julia Donaldson

Illustrated by Michael Terry

CHARACTERS

Elephant

Tiger

Mouse

Squirrel

Mole

Voice *(can also read stage directions)*

Scene 1

(Elephant, Tiger and Mouse are out for a walk. They come to a house.)

Elephant   Who lives in this house?

Mouse   My friend Squirrel lives here.

Tiger   Look, there's a notice on the door. What's that word beginning with R? Can you read, Elephant?

Elephant	Er, yes, but the sun is too bright today.
Mouse	I can read! The word is "Reward!"
Tiger	That sounds good! What else does the notice say?
Mouse	It says, "Are you big? Are you brave? Can you find the nuts in the cave?"

Elephant Well, that sounds easy. I'm big.

Tiger And I'm brave.

Elephant Let's find out more!

(They ring on the bell. Squirrel comes out.)

Mouse   Hello, Squirrel. What's all this about nuts in a cave?

Squirrel   Well, they're my nuts. I saved them in the cave last year. Now I'm hungry and I want to eat them.

Tiger   So why don't you go and get them?

Squirrel   I'm too scared. People are saying there's a monster in the cave!

Elephant   That doesn't bother me. I'm so big!

Tiger   It doesn't bother me either.
I'm so brave!

Elephant   Tell us about the reward. What is it?

Squirrel   It's a wonderful feast!

Elephant   That sounds good. I'll find those nuts for you, Squirrel.
In fact, I'll go right now.

Squirrel   Oh, thank you!

(Elephant waves goodbye.

On the way to the cave she meets Mole.)

Mole Hello, Elephant. Can you help me? I've got a thorn in my paw.

Elephant No, not just now. I'm in a hurry. I'm off to find the nuts in the cave.

Mole Do you know what to say to the monster in the cave?

Elephant No. What should I say to him?

Mole You have to shout, "I'M GOING TO GET YOU!"

Elephant I see. That sounds easy. Goodbye, Mole.

*(Elephant reaches the cave.
She looks inside and shouts.)*

Elephant I'M GOING TO GET YOU!

Voice I'M GOING TO GET YOU!
GET YOU! GET YOU!

Elephant Help! Help!

(Elephant runs back to Squirrel's house.)

Mouse Did you find the nuts, Elephant?

Elephant Er, yes, but I didn't have a bag to carry them in.

Squirrel Here's a bag.

Elephant Oh, yes, thank you, but I'm rather tired now.

Tiger   I'll go and find the nuts!
Squirrel   Thank you, Tiger!
You're so brave!

*(Tiger takes the bag and waves goodbye.
On the way to the cave he meets Mole.)*

Mole	Hello, Tiger. Can you help me? I've got a thorn in my paw.
Tiger	Not just now. I'm in a hurry. I'm off to find the nuts in the cave.
Mole	Do you know what to say to the monster in the cave?
Tiger	No. What do I have to say?
Mole	You have to growl, "I'M GOING TO EAT YOU!"
Tiger	I see. That sounds easy. Goodbye, Mole.

(Tiger reaches the cave. He looks inside and growls.)

Tiger   I'M GOING TO EAT YOU!
Voice   I'M GOING TO EAT YOU!
           EAT YOU! EAT YOU!
Tiger   Help! Help!

(Tiger runs back to Squirrel's house.)

Squirrel   Did you find the nuts, Tiger?

Tiger   Er, yes, and I put some of them in the bag. But on the way home I fell down, and the nuts rolled away.

Mouse   Oh dear! Will you go back for the rest?

Tiger   Well, I would, but I'm rather tired now.

Mouse   Shall I go and get them?
Elephant You? You're not big!
Tiger   And you're not brave!
Mouse   No, but Squirrel is hungry.
              He needs those nuts!
Squirrel   Thank you, Mouse. You're very kind.

Scene 2

(Mouse takes the bag and waves goodbye. On the way to the cave she meets Mole.)

Mole   Hello, Mouse. Can you help me?
              I've got a thorn in my paw.

Mouse   Of course I'll help you.
              It looks very sore.

(Mouse takes the thorn out of Mole's paw.)

Mole   Thank you. Now, perhaps I can help you. Where are you off to?

Mouse   I'm going to find the nuts in the cave.

Mole   Do you know what to say to the monster in the cave?

Mouse   No, what do I have to say?
Mole   You have to whisper,
            "I want to be friends with you."
Mouse   Thank you, Mole. I'll try that. Goodbye.

*(Mouse reaches the cave.
She looks inside and whispers.)*

Mouse   I want to be friends with you.
Voice   I want to be friends with you. With you. With you.

(Mouse finds the nuts in the cave and drags the bag back to Squirrel's house.)

Mouse   I found the nuts! Here they are.

Tiger   But what about the monster?

Mouse   I think he must be very shy. I heard some footsteps but I didn't see him.

Elephant   Perhaps he was scared of Tiger and me.

Mouse   Yes. You're so big and brave!

Squirrel Thank you, Mouse.
Now for the reward!

Tiger Oh good. What is it?

Squirrel It's a wonderful feast of nuts!

Elephant But I don't like nuts!

Tiger Neither do I!

Squirrel Oh dear! Do you like nuts, Mouse?

Mouse Yes, I love them!

Squirrel Good! Let's tuck in!

(Squirrel and Mouse eat the nuts. Elephant and Tiger look cross.)